AN INTERMITTENT MUSIC

An
Intermittent
Music

1975—2010

Ted Pearson

chax
2016

An Intermittent Music is a serial work comprising eighteen books in four
movements. Earlier versions of these books were published by Trike Books,
Origin, Square Zero Editions, Gaz, O Books, Roof Books, Un bureau sur
l'Atlantique, Zasterle Press, Meow Press, Past Tents Press, and Singing Horse
Press, gratefully acknowledged.

Cover Painting: Liubov Popova, *The Pianist*, 1915. Oil on canvas, 106.5 x 88.7
cm. Purchased 1966. National Gallery of Canada, Ottawa. Photo © National
Gallery of Canada.

ISBN 978 0 9862640 9 2

Chax Press is supported in part by the School of Arts & Sciences at the
University of Houston-Victoria. We are located in the UHV Center for the Arts
in downtown Victoria, Texas.

Chax acknowledges the support of graduate and undergraduate student interns
and assistants who contribute to the books we publish. In Fall 2016 our interns
are Julieta Woleslagle, Sophia Kameitjo, Errin Maye, and Gabrielle Delao.

This book is also supported by private donors. We are thankful to all of our
contributors and members. Please see http://chax.org for more information.

CHAX
P. O. Box 162
Victoria, TX 77902
http://chax.org

for Sheila Lloyd

O! learn to read what silent love hath writ:
To hear with eyes belongs to love's fine wit.

— Shakespeare

Contents

Topologies

Contingencies

Songs Aside

Encryptions

The Grit

The isolated man is dead

— George Oppen

1   Somehow
     it seems to destroy us

     sun   rock   sea

     these elements
     at the edge
     of a continent

     windswept

     there is a wearing down
     there is a wearing away

     there is a way

2   We remember
     but little
     of what led us here

     and are left

     with nothing
     beyond our ability
     to speak

     of these things

     among which
     we find ourselves
     undone

3   That rock
     which sun splits
     and sea turns
     to sand

     windswept

     the grit

     a wearing away

     body too
     to barer body
     so splits
     and turns

     turns to

     drifts

     and burns

4   To turn again
     to the live edge

     of that beach
     on which

     rock   shards   image

     of a life

the instant after
the mind breaks

albeit each shard
has its edge

and can draw blood

no blame

5   Beyond our ability
      to speak of these things

      the elements gather
      drift and burn

      terrigenous

      at land's end

      these bodies sunning
      the tide running

      back to the sea
      again

6   The children play
      near the rocks

      the young

men and women
walk about

in contrast with
their ripening

bodies

the lean expanse
of the sea

7   Driftwood

and the water's
rhythm

burden

of the water's
rhythm

and the couples

lie on their
blankets

staring out

8   Beauty's object
fuel for fire

at day's end
a man and a woman

rise as one
and stand apart

as if a couple
were nothing more

than any two
together

9   He reaches for her
    smiling
    at her beauty

    which is ample

    and so he thinks
    within reach

    hardly an embrace

    she neither yields
    nor resists

    seeming aware

    that his smile
    does not
    include her

10   Unable to proceed
      unable to keep out the world
      unable to include it

      in what they are
      they move apart

      and rejoin awkwardly
      at increasing intervals
      of time and of desire

      wearing down

      to a common discomfiture
      of flesh uncommonly
      exposed to the world

      in which that order
      of desire against which

      the elements are
      and can do nothing
      is not apparent

11   Walking directionless
      walking regardless

      unsure they can answer
      to where they are

      while gulls wheel
      overhead in setting

sunlight   wing
to wing tip turning

alternating light
and dark

12   Space
and what fills it

objects

of desire
borders

drive the eye

back
on itself

faces

reflected
in a tide pool

and the life

teeming
underneath

13   At a distance
the man and the woman
are a cell

dividing in the wide
body of the world

unaffected to the naked eye

between them
a landscape
is defined in which

the only growing thing
is distance

14   Deserted

though the man
stands

his ground

he is grown
a part of it

and cannot fill

the space
that assumes

his being there

and turns
the woman

turns away

her lithe back
to the sea

Reaped Figures

The dead are notoriously hard to satisfy

— Jack Spicer

1   Whose words gathered
described things   lies
naked and unforewarned

with equal intervals
without these things

a mind preoccupied with
less than thought
a tone when we are gone

2   And I kept myself from going mad
by singing to my body

what is your name   your maiden name
washed as the wind varies

3   Tired of appearance
and disappearance
he rearranges pain

there are no colors
words only   he regrets
that wreckage

4   Night's hard wages
paid on waking

I made my way
to the harbor

morning light's
renewal wretched

in lowering fog
salt air

a stinging wind
in my eyes

5   Impossible music
raveled and spun

whitecaps under
drifting echoes

bound to detail
the least disharmony

once unnoted
now unsung

6   Adrift in a world
     of words though words
     may fail and shadows

     reconstruct that world

     will one surrender
     self for love   look
     where the surface dances

     silvered by the wind

7   Too clean   on time

     some other flicker
     stirs the crowd

     without music

     what indolence supplies
     smoothing silk

     thighs

8   Naked

they are said to be
almost equal

who swayed

to the music
and stirred

with their hips

mindless   fecund
applause

9   I was in love then
and no mistake

but when I think about
what it was like

leave me alone

there were dances
guitars

10   Mournful stave
       of once-proud flesh

       now passive
       in strange beds

       forgotten details
       forgotten syntax

       nerves rooted
       in pretense

11   Long of tooth
       reft of claw

       late rising
       Dog Star howls

       the cunnilingual
       law

12   Without silence
is no gain   flesh apt
to no dexterity

sunlight fades

in the rustle of
drapes   closing
out the world

13   If every journey
ends in dreams

in dreams to whom
shall we answer

could words be found
in another climate

virgin with virgin
wine without headache

the songs between summer
and the sea's bulge

would avail us
when we reef

14   A thread of blue

to restore the light
is sufficient

a motive you can lay
your hands on

nothing is

but draws from a well
deeper than history

wakes where air
alight with sun

rises

15   Of all things
      no one living
      but flares

      and is lost

      the marvels
      scattered lines
      staggering

      empty at last
      unintelligible
      sleep   harbor

      no tide strains

      who sang of
      the sea and
      dry weather

Southern Exposure

for him everything is possible, except life

— E. M. Cioran

1   A dimensionless point   full stop
     from which all distinction flows

     yes yesterday   no today
     say what you will and prove it

     the silence the blind take for color is insoluble
     telling of danger the surface is askew

     as if every solid were a surface at rest
     or an object lesson to which we attest

     not even the words what we say they are
     almost the opposite   real   not quite

2   We have taken the shadow for the city
     and the knowledge for which it stands

     though boredom argues against deliberation
     the prospect opens to a kind of refulgence

     forgetting and forgetting one has forgotten
     the risk of exchanging light for warmth

     or the fact of love for its merest semblance
     the warmth   however sourced   benign

     wanting of place something more than mockery
     and make-work filing absolutes between harvests

3   Returning from labor through an air of weariness
this is the so-called instruction in the womb

the site of that estrangement inordinately mapped
what could come out of such wild rags

the toys and snapshots evidence of childhood
words and their shadows   faces   names

keyed to the curative properties of denial
familiar music fills a shuttered room

where children dream of hungry ghosts
and wake to unknown appetites

4   Order is the myth of history hollowed out
of a living past   a past half dead

as if anything native to this place could grow here
the whole grows accustomed to its missing parts

illusions   irritations   symptoms of decay
from infinite regression to infinite delay

the story comes to its own conclusion
impacted to retain a certain grace

in this house everything has its place
east is a direction   but not from here

5   He found the translation cryptic
     though many seemed eager for civil war

     mistaking the sight of blood for freedom
     denying the common heritage of flight

     quick to reject the specter of doubt
     but quicker to conjure winds and charms

     in which the present divines its future
     riddled with laws of cause and effect

     unspeakable now   who press so close
     the idea that anything was possible

6   Impelled as stars are not in their accord
     bitterness adorns the bare syllables

     letting love lie cognate with despair
     to speak of exile in native air

     timidity   stupidity   there are other explanations
     for wonder lost in a wealth of detail

     as if beauty were a creature's final protest
     the Sirens sing to a running tide

     while brainwaves break upon that shore
     where dreams of you abide

7   Caught between abandon and abandonment
a young man stands at the edge of a ditch

do you take what you can get? oh   do you get it?
yet absorbed because depth always absorbs

drawn to the image of her narrow breasts
remarking the brilliant plumage of the males

uselessly present in the general absence
seeing the better   following the worse

under the banner of the word *vast*
one is almost tempted to believe him innocent

8   Lovers move through his mind like rumors
impedimenta hidden in the shadows of the rushes

pure bands of color in brutal succession
and the heat   animate   intractable   fleshed

no harm in dreaming a chaste repose
the aromatic night still fresh on his hands

bound by the annihilating logic of nearness
a caress is a fist unfurled in the darkness

to trace the imprint of phantom limbs
on a bed where to be warm is to be false

9   The cult of the difficult exposed to desire
in a possible world   a possible order

though the subject is but a lapse in momentum
as far as things are concerned we may know them

where matter is mirrored in light of its motion
and the arc of becoming is more than a notion

of life played out across lines of sight
lest the mirror reflect something more than light

between evocation and direct perception
what remains is an image of the fact

10   Beyond knowledge and the reach of eyes
he watched at a window of his own making

the continuous flow of possible relations
in a physical world   intact and unobliged

not to describe the definitive features
it could be anywhere one looked out

breathing contradiction like a rare scent
pleased to accommodate the stillest nerve

one with the weight of surrendered things
a punishing reward at the end of the mind

The Blue Table

He speaks of himself as of another

— Samuel Beckett

1   What can our changes
     bring to the flesh

     who find ourselves
     at the seams
     of a country

     of ritual prisons
     of provocation

     cells from which
     the body of
     love cries out

     for a shape
     to contain its dreams

2   Assume courage
     assume the continuing

     struggle for freedom

     and the burden
     of proof

     offer a starving child
     your breast

     a mad dog

     a long cool drink
     of your body

3   Improvident
whose form is torture

the constancy

of her denial of
his desire grown

useless against her

image   taut
with thought

of her nipples

remembered
taste of her

hard nipples

the kind of evidence
one hesitates

to admit

4   And the room's air
     thick with odors

     long body

     would you know it
     if you saw it

     cool body

     snowball in hell –
     an assumption

     of the beginning

     words are not
     to be believed

5   Dreams are stones

     the song he is singing
     carries no weight
     beyond what is sung

     these are his lips

     they are cracked
     they are caked with blood
     he is spitting blood

     he is singing his song

44

6   Rubble

the common lot
vacant

abandoned

where gathering
gathers talk

of the weather
talk of the town
and the streets

bordering
this desolated

stratum

unrelieved
weight

from above

7   Unlikely

as it seems
the years

carry over

the past
rendered

past rendering

impoverished
rendering

of love

that terrible
word

8   Pure spectacle

    yet beyond what is
    there is still something else
    that happens

    hardly a covenant

    though the heart opens
    as at the beginning
    of a perilous journey

    travel light

    intimate knowledge
    at the ends of nerves
    the end of speech

9   The blue table
     is not absolute

     but a figure
     drawing attention

     from the difficult
     events in the room

     in which it stands –

     so one imagines
     being held

     from despair
     by a common object

     an object held
     if nothing else

     in common

10   If it needed saying
      it got said

      if you sit here
      long enough

      nothing happens

      this is the interval
      where silence fills

      what love has failed
      to accomplish

Ellipsis

Intensity is silent. Its image is not.

— René Char

I   The script is indecipherable

a language bound
in beauty and in strangeness
to the eye

a foreign language

not our language

though behind it a brilliant
light the color of
blood rushing in arousal

as to a fresh wound shines

2   Emmetropic

yet in that light

intimate
substitutions
occur

your hair
becomes her
hair

the odor
of your dampness
her odor

your amplitude

hers

3   What goes
by the name
of love is

banishment

nothing
out the window

no window

world in which
denying this

difficult love

we mistake
its language
for our own

4   In every telling
is the half forgotten

horror vacui

whose lips

to resist
these pages

parted

silence

our mother
tongue

5   Half earth
     half lightning

     desire

     rises and is
     received

     thus to equilibrate

     the eternal
     variant

     caught

     in common
     time

6   That which is divided
     in itself yields

     a remainder   thought's

     intricate measure
     lost in person place and thing
     the moving parts

     of a parting begun

     when the lyric breaks
     the song is sung

7   Not the embrace

but the encounter
is decisive

continuity

the union of
unlike things

language

that I spoke in
script in which

I wrote

Refractions

days we die / are particular

— Robert Creeley

1   In designs   love

dawn the phase
the mind addressed
blossoms

life like light
proposes this

anew where
things illumine the
periphery

now in sight

2   Seldom a song

the leaves the breeze
stiffens scrape

an interior

defined   plate glass
through which

a rainbow breaks

3   Incognito
the return of the sun

though memory
slights
or plunges

to fit meaning
to the heat

4   Irreversible

that part
which looks

unflinching
at the sun

departing

as it looks
unloved   if

it is loved
unless

it is loved

5   Given
     the moon

     a fist

     the glass

     illumines
     the garden

     ruins

     the mind

6   Difficult
     as ever

     to speak
     of paradise

     without
     reference

     a solid
     describes

7   Appearances

     to the contrary
     anything

     is possible

     she who loves me
     loves me not

     wanting anything

     as easily leads
     to wanting

     anything else

8   The balance
     the song

     the blossom

     in time
     petals rust

9   The custom
     is to speak
     of beauty

     idle hints
     in other words

     to oppose to
     all events
     of whiteness

     senses
     apprehending

10   Deflected
     sunlight glints
     in eyes

     a glimpsed
     surmise

     of the shore
     from which
     where it sets

     the generic
     recedes

11   Matter
      like convention
      impedes

      sight

      stripped
      momentary
      world

12   So real
      you'd think she was

      dancing

      although of the spirit
      we could say

      with Mencius

      it is rather difficult
      to describe

13   Whose voice
has led to music

thighs

to startled
thought

defying gravity

flowers stem
and root

as brain

from root
arose

in thought

a flower more
to be desired

14   Old song

tune
in the head

lyrics

intermittent
voice

of a dead

time
an immensity

mind alone

this
obliquity

gaps

15   Not to record

          the elapsed intensity
          but the fact

          of not seeing

          in the morning light
          airs as words

          are given

16   Voluptuous hours
          no doubt

          the interplay
          subtler
          the mind still

          receding from

          its dreams of you
          reveals at dawn
          that sleepers too

          collaborate
          in what goes on

17   Garden

of annuals
but no

garden

plot at least
the play

of light

through the
window

can be seen

as the plot
foretold

18   Lit by love
      the ontic rift

      thrives

      as if one
      might survive

      the depths

      from which
      in her eyes

      lights

      arise   over
      the remains

      of love

19   In time my companion
      you will move on
      and elsewhere rise

      to greet the dawn
      in solitude

      that lovely power
      and at peace
      if ever I pleased you

20   Melody
      forbears the rest

      a gauntlet of air

      anatomy

      the streets

      nerves an assertion
      of the not done

21   Life like light
      but the light fails

      and the life

      its ardor damped
      to confound

      credibility

      a difficult figure
      to ground

22   Slow to arrive
      quick to remove

      from the vale
      to the void
      to which we all

      return as forms
      of matter prove

23   Simply a figure
      cut in time

      the only available fabric

      that which
      from out of itself

      stands

      somehow
      out of place

24   To begin again
      is no gain

      unless in wonder
      to construct a frame
      of mind wherein

      the relation between
      this music and that
      release which mercy's

      quotient time
      anneals is seen

25   From level ground
      hard ground
      broken to descend

      cords in a neck

      unused to labor
      irrational numbers
      practical skills

      more than abstraction

      these forms meant
      limits   bold ratios
      of light impose

26 Echoes bodied
 forth curve
 back in bounded space

   ending baffled
   save that time

   assembled brightens
   into solids

   conscious
   almost lifeless
   knowing

27 Enharmonic

   sight and sound
   fading exact
   a reply

   but nothing
   is exchanged

   that can be
   tuned in
   or translates

   two alike

28   Of those
      long hours

      wherein
      the stars

      compel
      no feeling

      beyond
      the absence

      of feeling
      there is

      no mystery
      the mind

      cannot mistake
      for misery

29   Epistemology

      the worm in the apple
      duration itself

      a form of dread

      the profound sleep
      of objects

      for example

      false access
      to eternity

30   With discipline
      the mind turns
      quickly from fear

      to leap not measure

      to imagine itself
      something other
      if not more than

      that which

      having taken
      thought   remains
      its own effect

31   An ordinary mind

          uncharted   gray   given
          life as it might be lived

          out of the running

          simply to observe
          the least wind disposed

          at crossroads to omens

          instructions the figure
          at the window awaits

32   Then spring
          in the mirror yields
          by what art

          the rhythm of waves

          the white landscape
          the absent one
          the departure of

          memory   rain   insomnia

          unnatural blossoms
          in a three-story house
          with basement

33   Music plays low

        in the next room
        in a different story

        in another life

        as she dances
        she throws off

        whatever

        she's wearing
        and is barely there

        shown there

        swaying
        at a distance

34   In air as on paper

          each word gathered
          in the changing light

          in a kind of garden

          is a kind of ghost
          careless love

          unfathomably wakes

          and blends with
          her in cadence

35 This last
    is closed in you

    her face

    older

    in the end
    flowers

    in the mind

    aflame
    yet drawing

    pleasure

    out
    of a flame's

    duration

Coulomb's Law

there remained in the midst of the losses,
this one thing: language

— Paul Celan

1   At three removes the blue world
    plies its rounds if love applies
    whence we are born   head first
    you can see it in our eyes

2   Mutable fire out of vernal seed
    arrives ensouled at solstice
    by fate inured to darker days
    lightning elides lightening

3   From fevered dream to episteme
    culture conjures a willing host
    Le Prince du Printemps (his legend)
    hangs you up the most

4   All the available evidence is awkward
    always venery and hungry glances
    up from under   the moaning rises
    matins of a sphere in heat

5   Legs in silk   a sound effect
    sudden glamour in a working port
    whose hips define the daily grind
    vision's material   eyes

6   With a hint of a smile
     a ghost of a chance   tough lodging
     for any dream   her lips open
     to take the air

7   A first glance spurs an obbligato
     of nerves guarded to survive
     a poverty of means   the evidence
     if you weren't   wasn't

8   Café grasp   restrained desire
     syntax with a view   corpse
     and mirror   land's end   remote
     in order to relate anew

9   Hazard courts enigmas in season
     the blossom in the sun in the cage
     a tight rope on a crying jag
     turned the corner   bent the page

10   Suspect motives diminish depth
     whose surface stems arousal
     like but not the charm of a true naïf
     a nude (in a sweat) stretched

11   Frames inter inanimate things
in the eye of a neural storm
restless particles wave en route
to forms content in forms

12   Blue angels   mock heroics
workers sun their ankles at lunch
drop-top dreams of weekend schemes
sex in a four-wheel drift

13   City limits   sleep cycles   frayed nerves
versus metal fatigue   arpeggiated wonders
body and soul   the celebrated
pleasures of the mouth

14   Demotic dissonance   odes' modes
a vamp ranging latitudes of voluntary color
pissant blues at the hop

15   Locals levitate to glib dub
scratch and sniff at the bar and grill
old-school jams on a scenic cruise
after hours   bop de ville

16   Last Call fills the empty streets
      of a world that waits in reflected glory
      for dawn to rouse that sun of ours
      and light the light of our lives

17   Brick window   glass house
      neighborhoods tourists never see
      the gesture is empty but what could fill it
      tympanum   distant thunder

18   Day for night   a model paradox
      hopes to forget appearances   old schisms
      over petty rituals   epiphenomena
      frequent as sleep

19   Susurratin' rhythm   hints of the hawk
      full moon quartered by oak leaves' sway
      or the hound heard baying at the half moon
      rising weeks later over Half Moon Bay

20   Backstreets parallel the main drag
      empire tours   local tongue
      where what you hear is all you've heard
      there is no solution to this lyricism

21 Voices in a crowd   a crowd's voice
    each raised to the power of one
    stretching the known   makes a melody
    hand and eye construe

22 Taxonomy wounds the least detail
    home remedy   white on white
    conjuring difficult you at the buzzer
    a feral tongue off the rim

23 For *cant* read *zounds*   cute dupe
    fandango under the drain
    starlight Nembutal arriba plankton
    trellis a working brain

24 Bold with appetite   la bella donna
    roves giving tongue   but a sharp one –
    then with a snap of topiary grillwork
    the urban garden closes

25 Hatteras passage   white flag
    false start with ruler and English
    first souvenir   no torso green
    fools figure in book by the sea

26   Wed for water splits stone
whose course is map's relief
inaction's axiom   ars longa
deigns to cipher rain's brief

27   Thinking reed   whose music abstracts
thought as work in song enacts
what distance covers   measure strictly is

28   Means are extremes if sight is love
to express this body   raise it
personal effects (question of degree)
to define means   our extremes

29   Years vault an acre's wager
to paradise   staves   of trees broken
into rounds weathering
in high grass

30   Stumped   one can imagine skies
to look to whatever makes this stand
unsought (for witness) a remainder

31   Raised grain praised plane
variations on a cord of wood
after images literally vanish
what is between the rest is good

32   Occipital libretti   water hammer
hammers water motor gong –
the aberration of these phrases in a cloud
sunset with plaster cast

33   Blues betide our lives by the water
from stillborn dreams to migrant bliss
wanting anything easily leads
to wanting more than this

34   Wide skies foreground
billowed heads   solo pillowed
on grassy bed   whiffing
spring in the buds

35   Heady player leaps in
to be or not to bop   but whether
velocity equals veracity
summit   thin air

36   Drills traverse the quiet lane
       sidewalk assessment   droll spit
       suburb of silt   generic beer
       kiss that reveals the teeth

37   Between the tidings of evil sailors
       and the tempo of small blessings
       the goddess of punishing choices reclines
       by a fire too soon gone out

38   Poste restante   her billets-doux
       muta d'accento   trobar clus
       ties that bind a thousand silences
       deaf ears   alluvial fans

39   In Colombia the rolling pin
       is a sign of marital bliss
       what one wonders would they make
       of the goodwife's nightly tryst

40   Life unravels its storied threads
       from war to war and the names of
       women   no Greek weaver here

41   Incontrovertible   with the top down
      white noise poised in a cold snap
      smug gums cradle snug guns
      cross fire raking leaves of grass

42   Maladroit reflex stunts grip
      in the gap between names and things
      where the sun is a rose but coarsely
      wove   branded thus unriddled

43   Local knowledge   off the tracks
      lifts a glass to all it lacks
      and holds it high till the ice cracks

44   *Divorce* wrote the doctor *a sign
      of the times*   embodied in fucking
      atop the clothing   laid out
      to be packed by morning

45   Reckoning a wreck   blown rose
      from first light to the last word   scraps
      desire for trinkets

46   Strange to have come to two
when one had come to none
in some languages it is not possible
to say sit in the sun

47   Functional polymers   tribal bonds
the body lost in thought
mass but bits that shine uncut
old it equal to nought

48   Mossy lintel   seen
but not heard through the wind
chimes   the song is you

49   Folly beach   highway tango
untitled study for skin device
tuned to the timbrels and bold trombones
that sack the city with say-so

50   Up keeps aired out   housebound leaps
to wild yonder   tracking licks on old disks
increasingly evanescent phenomena

51   Cronies call for chronic hits
　　　　road noise melds to open air
　　　　cantus firmus　the wind in the wires
　　　　bird lending lilt in scale

52   Split shift (sly sex) opens
　　　　the lexicon to plea or please
　　　　raised letters on the sidewalls
　　　　stutter in a turbid breeze

53   Of others a bevy in lieu of you
　　　　stones in my passway　stoned on the street
　　　　pulse a proxy of mere locale
　　　　frieze of many climates

54   Gonadology　jitterbug waltz
　　　　rebar struttin' with a lead-pipe cinch
　　　　stone declines hypothetical ground
　　　　to know Veronica in a pinch

55   Rough trade eyes sweet meat in dishabille
　　　　quantum youth faces end of all tricks
　　　　sidereal atrocities nailed to the expanse
　　　　a montage fixed on gender

56   Origami bookwork   random flights
      sheer gumption of deponent squat
      a line as on a map   hormonal bleats
      a capella in a vacant lot

57   Dark ages   light years
      parsecs parsed by argent ears
      poets too once glossed these skies
      at night with naked eyes

58   The narrative founders on mythic scarps
      cantilevered sunrise   skewed proof
      thought without pedigree picks a bone
      with fossils from the late prosaic

59   Found objects found alive   figments
      of a mind (all but gone)   wretched acoustics
      the wind flourishing   no matter
      what scraps dreaming slams home

60   Fantasies common to childhood include
      the orphan with an unknown but fabulous destiny
      the poem is something else   the poem
      would include him if it could

61   In the exile's dream of the open road
when the light changes the spectrum shifts
enough to recall the shades of home
but not to slow his outbound drift

62   Though lyrics fade the melody persists
inveterate biology   a blue funk
with every loophole barred to its exponent
even doubt is carnal

63   Futurity mocks the history of defeat
fierce winds scatter ancestral airs
from lithic dreams to extant glyphs
of lives neither here nor there

64   Anonyms of light and sound
native plants   in a row   in the ground
roots   diabolus in musica

Mnemonics

Aboli bibelot d'inanité sonore

— Stéphane Mallarmé

1   Through scattered realms the moon lights cells
    a single vagrant bloom
    obscure at first   male and female
    opposite   the prism

2   One bright fire   attendant shade
    the rime usurps the hearth

3   With aspect bent to written lore
    living memory survives the descent
    ranging its old enclosures

4   From leaf to spangled multitude
    no surface sleeps with logic
    dawn's gray eminence   mist that woos
    the fervor of local spirits

5   Mere topography   seismic menace
    lightning reconciled to chance cadences
    the known habits of every seed

6   Diligent cells   the truly primitive
     weight of beauty at anchor

7   From the plunge   millennia
     from the window   miles of beach
     glacial traces delimit the breach
     the mist elaborates the road

8   Leaving much unvisited to trace the ways
     first love   an unvoiced stop
     from point to line to plainest speech
     furled in fetal bliss

9   At ship's prow   ancestral stock
     a motley inscribed in a single stroke
     to grace at landfall a musical note

10   Mechanism of altered air
     renewal's dowry   equinoctial dare
     the threshold pulse empowers rimmed
     collation's spell dispelled

11 The clouds are thesis and plenitude
  to baffle heaven's hosts
  with beauty and estrangement
  a stipend fit for ghosts

12 Bedclothes bristle with jargon for brickwork
  body with candor matter in ink

13 A scratched surface to prove any point
  reflects the wreck of days
  endured however bitter the measure
  of waste and a steady gaze

14 Seen from shore the storm unfolds
  its briefest bloom to a public world
  the sexual bloom overwhelming the walls
  of a city ransomed to the least threat

15 Urgent perhaps for the last time
  even in hell the dead keep busy
  burnishing all thought of you
  until memory retains the exact shade

16   Haint's grisaille   labial tint
       damped promise of calcined gates
       talk stemmed to a stalk of silence
       the music conjugal and frozen

17   Death by bewilderment   clairvoyant age
       to evoke a pastoral sympathy
       for stuff of dumb indifference made

18   Root clump under marsh water
       the water itself a duration weaving
       light and dark in the wind's wake
       as the current flows out of sight

19   Wavelets run in the tules
       where thought is but a ploy
       the exercise of the analytic
       rooted in excess of joy

20   A singular music whose every part
       seeming one (being many) proves none
       idle sums to excuse all counting
       sung of successive suns

21   Alternations of form and flux
     figure more than speech
     the curvature of the earth for example
     or the mind staved in by lucidity

22   Rogue conduction goes to ground
     flared ganglia bent to the trace
     after hours   a recurring dream
     peoples the dark with visible things

23   Blues in the night   second sight
     near or vast as an eye

24   Scattered glints of captive weather
     taunt sleep with cunning flutter
     silent tongues' untenable cartage
     duns the optic ache

25   Limits fall to proof adduced from
     shards of sorties past   the arduous path
     surrounded by (stippled with) pinnacles
     that emphasize the vanished mass

26   Could time be reconciled to memory's intent
       desire might lie with it   content

27   From trance to the garden of stones
       at tunnel's end the apocryphal light
       without warmth or known source
       subsumed by endless night

28   An ear to an era to hear each year
       perpends wed ages to allay its fear
       for old airs lost among welcome new
       whose unsung pages plight our rue

29   The wind in the wires is also song
       of which no words survive
       nor want of such inconstancies
       as bid one's own to thrive

30   Let guest be host at ghost's behest
       sung heights stressed by ice and fire

31   Stalled borealis trembles to recount
       the drift that measures prevented crystal
       perpetuity exacting a creature of air

Catenary Odes

By wire, by wing, by wind, by chance

— Eugenio Montale

1 At home and not in paradise
   purview   the wild iris

   hardpan pipes a pygmy forest
   believe I'll dust my broom

2 The art of poverty could boast broad dominions
   esteemed colors   scarce glory

   beating time to the goon ictus
   onyx   mamboid   eschatology

3 Presumption suckles fact from matrix
   the cleft path to free will

   anechoic   (the) devouring din (the)
   technology exists to record

4 Of flesh bereft on successive nights
   phantom lovers vary by the dream

   sleep's surrogate scrolls the continuum
   memory vamps to   unpretending time

5   Symmetries of the innate sentence
the trial by error the period ends

blameless seed of endowed tropics
uncertain transit   essential oils

6   Who most mistake the real forgive it
crosstown traffic   island life

each thing equal to the shape of its moment
dressing Edenic meat

7   Not by volume but whiff of death
withal too faint to prove

more than a field   the generic groove
thick with civil solids

8   Distance balks coherent mirrors
the glad day publishes grief between tears

anode   the body electric in a brownout
the western mind in a jar

9   Groove's recompense is outside time
     where pulse is pure conjecture

     the darker art's to hear with eyes
     that eyes might own their sparkle

10   The thawed harp weirds its figments of prattle
     toothsome sexemes   a quire of rags

     whose plaint unnerves unbroken ground
     lashed to the vernal rush

11   Animate angels at inclement angles
     beggar speech while on the wing

     in the hum of parallel signs that sing
     the first insinuation was amorous

12   Memory's cult occludes its cargo
     rank encumbrance   risible stone

     reluctant latitudes of absolute repeal
     matter's pastorale

13   Blackbirds drunk on pyracantha
      limpid stints of sun

          eyes otherwise drawn to the annular
          antics of heavenly bodies

14   Hunger feeds the deforming flame
      and lost estate of play

          the capacious admits a qualified plural
          who come but seldom stay

15   What strange certitude subs for the thrash
      of a discontinuous world

          galactic noise beyond the verge
          of a prosody thus unfurled

16   Zoned in a prospect lit with names
      duty's discourse is dust to dust

          morning's device   a surety of light
          radiant amidst the miserable atoms

17   Stunned keys hammer intransitive seasons
      under the aspect of numbered stars

      whose labile light defines the night
      as the void that fools call heaven

18   Day of wrath   day of sorrow
      each next day a death deferred

      the slow tongue's stab at reportage
      to limn the sweet unheard

19   Lies splintered from perjured heaven
      speak to the whole these figures mend in us

      half carrion   half specter   the catalogue
      raisonné   the lives of the poets

20   The affairs of infinite tradition elate rare strains
      of fictitious blossoms   nude (under all that

      stitchery) reascends a stairway to the stars
      hips' syncopation   fatback drums du temps

21   The past stands clear of present pain
the plot prefers the spreading stain

a confusion of motives   sole precedent
despair as a second language

22   Lost loves winnowed in memory's tray
bespeak a history of gaps and flows

where each next beat affirms the will
to live is a matter of blood

23   Pleasure is not a common name
wind over low ground   not this world

dawn's unattainable pink decries
the prose of windows and doors

24   Oxides tint the lingering cirrus
blacktop traces the coastal spine

now even the horizon is a pun
swept and glossed by the sun

25 Pickleweed   mud flats   tidal aroma
    accretion of wind   wings and sails

    picture a child conversant with raptors
    in those pleasant fields

26 Tides compound the sea's sum
    seeming is believing   wave upon wave

    to write paradise   solve for stone
    impalpably arrayed

27 Prodigal ease offends the peace
    elemental blank collects its future

    lately recalled from internal exile
    to effect a regime's demise

28 Death touches the air in the blood
    fellows the chanting dust

    whose process is continual
    entropic night and rust

29   Caprice athwart the divine inert
change alone exempts desire

from content's bondage to infant joy
hale in a climate of defeat

30   Payback looms with strings attached
bent to the fret and slant of fact

here these remnants sift untrammeled
ghosts of denial too firm to retract

31   Distant courtship's blighted troth
suborned by lust's intent

the roster of possibles hefts light
riven from its fundament

32   Desire   the mute with garrulous hands
describes a verbal embrace

of cause and consequence   lock and key
to provisional moments of grace

33   Born to arrogate fair moon
       heels locked at the nape

       horizontal orisons rose over tide surge
       ions strewn in the brume

34   A gendered phrase transects the void
       to the count of lunar days

       the subject (matter's rhythm) logged
       to chart the airs of its ways

35   Hard liquor and a sense of loss
       because you cannot live without your shadow

       somehow music   the end of a trope
       to signify where blood has been spilled

36   A little madness goes a long way
       and a history of loving strange women

       scaling the beds of ancient lakes
       crustal forces   badlands

37   The continuity (it follows) had been shattered
      a world we call it   but not the details

      grammar suffers the fatality of the given
      the forms we are (lost in them) known by

38   Summoned to recant   condemned to forget
      all cause ministers to power of place

      in the mind an incense beyond credibility
      to smoke out thoughts of home

Descant

Départ dans l'affection et le bruit neufs

— Arthur Rimbaud

1   Her sum each mute blue scape welcomes
    isocracy weathers its id for the nonce
    eroded omens of the upraised surface
    adrift in the age's othering

2   Stat conk is no-win kin to prove
    the *to be* too avers or errs
    as what once rove to grammar's tap
    root's dower divvied did endow

3   Eyes' ire augured in added hours
    a tantrum's trope avulsed
    the trumped shill gloms a reet demean
    or semblance of nought in vacuo

4   Loci linked by hectic metal
    chords course nerve-borne the finite rush
    to table time   to ear   to ink out earth
    its pastness   a last vast dig

5   Aeolic anthems adumbrate their fate
    beneath the backlit dust of stars
    from subsided tumuli to terminal moraine
    an epoch's unmarked grave

6   Censured   a nubile graph outwits
the veil of wickered axēs
leaving once-thralled staves bereft
of tessitura's troth

7   White heat fretted to blue changes
faith too flawed to hold love in it
behind closed doors an agon's ambit
antiquity's ageless weather

8   Cold steel tokes the god of rust
mud bone and jade   the unchained glacier
depth incumbent on actual years
some greet   others count   or hide in

9   The word stem spirals clockwise from
its rubric   a constancy of tombed roots
whence the entropic crystal of art
whose cleavage is its requiem

10   Minims limn the simplest intangibles
the pure word glosses the fulgent blade
posthumous memoirs   the isms be damned
that sparkle   in your eyes   is gone

11   Breath equivocates where once it praised
      ancestors grown remote as lore
      grammarians leashed to lamp the score
      by periplum   tongue to boot

12   Rules of thumb reap moot stumps
      wrath's ordnance mimes its flaws
      so that the ruined sanctuary gains
      the labor of a thousand gods

13   The ogive offsets occulted lots
      hindsight's slash and burn
      at terminal velocity the twig of fate
      whose lauds a wry child learns

14   Complicit night gone wild with wastage
      venture foliage adorns the lily
      mated and abated   the physics of denial
      in a weave of works and wonder

15   Bared to the windrows' chronic rune
      a tune more hard than silent grows
      where neither thought nor word escape
      the thorns of its compass rose

16   Standing waves redact the light
      less world than loci an ardor compounds
      to each its shade or living shard
      the bitter alms of disregard

17   Conjuration's bride derides
      what ill wind ciphers as licensed heaven
      the elided illogic of Narcissus paired
      alien gaze and pulse

18   Anatomies crave their demon phases
      all zones yoked to rote thighs
      not that it lasts   uncommon child
      unasking and unaxed

19   A blood moon rises over ancient walls
      migratory qualms   unlettered bacchanals
      where nary a debriefed devil dare defile
      this diaspora of sun-seared nerves

20   Canticles court the biosphere
      from airborne Eros to inner ear
      where graphic bits abrade the font
      of rime's consoling matrix

21   Epic intervals filter quicks
      in situ fill a flogged fool's air
      breasting fire to clear what cause
      unsanctioned hungers there

22   Amply vexed if audile thought
      concedes the law   divines the circle
      deems the eristic hiss of logs
      a discourse sans parole

23   Twilight's garden is ever apt
      to harbor hues from a dying star
      homing through the bluest hour
      its fated template to embrace

24   The many cleave to the what of one
      quiet for an ocean   still for an air
      this conjugal blossom   these sceptered radii
      whose meridian senses gloried in

Planetary Gear

Everything vanishes, nothing is left
But space, the stars, and the singer.

— Osip Mandelstam

1   A world lost   a world unsuspected
    a song beginning *to continue* rises
    even as the whip hand rises
    to stave or augment the occasion

2   Old gods fettered to old gods' eyes
    disuse belies their works and wonders
    good and gone   the lot of them home
    to end their days alone

3   You say you can take or leave these streets
    much as those before you did
    or said they could and didn't because
    it sufficed for them to say so

4   From chance encounters of unlike things
    a melody emerges   estranging and estranged
    immune to the call of harmonic Meccas
    whose chords would accord it concordance

5   I began as none other   the figure drawn
    was this figure   perhaps to recall
    how it came to be here   by the window
    in the evening   as the blinds were drawn

6   Who so rutted could fail to explain
how the road here leads to the road back
beyond the poses of delinquent weather
into what pride's remnants reckon

7   Particular days in a strange land
in winter the form imposed is long
particular words but no one's own
and no less particular song

8   Bitter cold it was and is
amidst these aspirants loath
to admit their provenance
blind to the fact of it

9   Not for nothing is the verb *to be*
given spirit enough or time
the thing itself   a contrivance
sanctuarial ebb of the sea

10   Restless variants   otherwise adrift
inhabit the sentiment of form
within whose bounds they think to find
shelter from the storm

11   Remote devices   mano a mano
        convene to conjoin their passion's flower
        and their lack's implacable demon

12   In the baleful stare of aftermath
        inconstant relics of consent
        unprepossessing and damned forthwith
        the hell of it utterly spent

13   A child's garden of uncertainty spans
        swollen acres of virgin ground
        O fractal mood resigned to conclude
        a goof or graciousness of love surely

14   The brickbats of legend unduly mouth
        their mothering frags in heat
        such duty-free booty to have lived so long
        on the sunny side of the street

15   Syntax of place divulges the outward
        skin compounded of all that is difficult
        lost in coincident waves that break
        and rootless make up ground

16   A song of the sign but not so simply
      to define the anterior edge of time
      where none precede the one in tangent
      nor otherwise grace its line

17   A rumored anything but random dark
      surrounds the world's trial sum
      left unsated as befits its fated medium

18   No longer young nor yet quite old
      whose passing gaze declines with age
      an end foretold by wont or pyre
      where found things waken under fire

19   Wired to the was of its slated plot
      the guttered pulse of a shuttered other
      proposed in song a song to be
      reprised in superfluity

20   A shadow world of hope deferred
      or spared the pleasure of living hands
      these old walls scoured in defeat

21   They are stories are they not
      these fabled errants of
      cloudless night   virtual heaven
      odds-on paradigms

22   Novae flex for the void they cozen
      tempered strange to common ends
      crazed sacramentals   light without heat
      true doubles   limned   forfend

23   Each bit prophesies stone proper
      to its orbit the world tacitly redounds
      to sounds like music makes

24   Triads tithe iconic sections
      bred in nascent rifts of sight
      sun-swept motes of shed effects
      filter down in earthly delight

25   Escalated music   endless steps
      tensors sited in vocal folds
      spur their plaint to the ragged edge
      our sorrows to condole

26   The pigment rests on its palette
      for want of what's not there
      while hand and eye draft substance
      from what words were and where

27   Ever another and an other come
      to please and to be pleased
      detailing thus unwearied lust
      a hardness reft of ease

28   With no thought of the road
      save you are on it   grammar likewise
      devolves on want and wants
      what it wants   don't ask

29   Flesh and bone   an old saw
      left in the traces equally worn
      and sung (if at all) if it cuts

30   Under tattooed skulls the color of legend
      hips rippled to an unheard beat
      while the star-struck night in full retreat
      did glister and surround me

31 No good trick derides its mount
    in or out of skew   nor
    does it reckon as indiscretion
    whole days lost in you

32 Circumstance dances to its own defining
    the incised vantage of impatient flesh
    on margin each bloom reseeds on hiatus
    a motley of endless arrivals

33 Inscriptions furrowed in fond purlieus
    whose letters cleave to their gradient
    athwart the sun's euphoric bent
    to shade each form in kind

34 Under leaden skies the trees grow bare
    within a circumference of heavy weather
    here as always already there

35 Alone together on a crowded stage
    the fourth wall bares the life we share
    till lightning strikes the set

36   Minor chords   primeval notes
         as if to voice the dead
         in the sting of morning fingers pluck
         by rote what's left unsaid

37   A door barred by sudden others
         their sum the measure of a thing like that
         and their song a bedlam sans merci
         of obligatory weekends in madness

38   Cells in division decline such rest
         as fairly breathes despair
         to bestir a breeze of like unease
         within the dissembling air

39   Xenobodacious winds displace us
         who with a leg up from Eden lope
         to the god-thang of our youth
         and joy and there await our fate

40   Earth's subaltern charms disdain
         the cartographer's passion for the demimondaine
         he has splayed as his compass rose

41   Parafoibles and bijouterie
adorn the heterology
of those whose I's historicize
the mind's obliquity

42   Random access deplodes the bricoleur
hand-carved shadows knock on wood
indeed we do   as you do too
whose hoodoo we adore

43   The fog of war obscures the stars
over ancient scars a tissue of longing
and rivers of unholy commerce

44   Canceled gravity unearthed remains
a tide starved for mere furtherance
at daybreak on the adamantine natch

45   From the chief viscera to the four winds
up late with early bird
later samplings zoned on the daybed
microtonic word

46   Atomized flagellants cant their plaints
     and ply amidst this widowed thicket
     drumabolic ruses

47   A lame god in glad rags
     fashions honey from the bitter grasses
     duly anointed my worthy constituents
     watch the eagle fly

48   Heritable shards shout down accumulation
     enough is enough   the interminable subject
     and the grail of a durable good

49   Sources cited beyond glass panes
     on the street the dialects of wind and rain
     to redress a moment's heat

50   The millennium essays its lyric accretions
     of angels in equipoise   graveyard sex
     and changelings thralled to the counter hex
     of a moonlit rut in hegira

51   Snake hips wail to a planetary jam
      while a rose in heat aspires to its scent
      and the updraft takes you higher

52   Dap stats rue unsighted vitals
      sweet talk guts the imperial will
      the cosine diddles cloven proof
      intestate flowers wag

53   Animate edges of the urban oblique
      honed on known if ravaged odds
      logoísmo swacked on morphemes
      shackled plangent to the regs verdad

54   Vicissitudes galore in drag minor
      preclude safe passage over strewn leaves
      hidden amidst autumnal mists
      the threat of winter's interdiction

55   A simple art in the execution
      amps its ardor up to defend
      factored seconds against the flames
      untended fires portend

56 Mother Time in a wilderness voiced
  the residuum an earth age
  imaged in ash and a ravening
  lust for profits

57 Trust-fund babies dance entranced
  under starry fitments to entropic beats
  while day-wage wraiths in dishabille
  hump till they're dead on their feet

58 Canny hours becalm the course
  the old sod runs to blooded ground
  whose limbic source in libidinal troves
  gets lost before it's found

59 Syntax sutures somatic glyphs
  to subsistence coded as time's interregnum
  awash in eternity's rain

60 Trauma maps the impolitic venues
  kinship staked on the road to hell
  the seductive inertia of real numbers
  riding high on a tidal swell

61   Sea wrack laps the last domain
at issue an epoch of rooms and views
opacities dubbed from their own excess
to a music box of blues

62   Of mechanic hours and a terminal sun
this sedimentary journal logs and flaunts
the griefs and grievances
our habitus haunts

Acoustic Masks

A new music is a new mind

– William Carlos Williams

1   Belief in structure
             is *as if*

                      from bedrock straight
                              to venereal soil

              home to the hum
                    of such spent things

                          whose every feature
                              speaks

2   What words are
             that others aren't

                      tracks per diem
                            prize quarks

              modal predations
                    drawn to scale

                      a bootleg turn
                          at dawn

3   Nor cloistered stint
          nor streetable flair

               suffice to render
                   la vie ordinaire

         clarity aside
            this is not a window

               or still life etched
                   in penumbral air

4   By fate distempered
          a cleft hook's barb

               echoes a ruined
                   music clings

         the specular posse
            closes in

               to dust the idiom
                   Beautiful Thing

5 Cathexis jubilates
   erotic octaves

     at the arc of the culminant
      ruby lips

   all claims rightly
    fluxed anon

     in the evangelical
      sway of hips

6 Reduced stock
   the cattle of the sun

     a proxy mated to
      love pro tem

   one man's heat
    is another's chill

     in the mythic
      bar and grill

7   Market forces
             a phallic knockoff

                   or piece of the true x
                         for which solve

            favored of the gods
                  Null and Void

                         by your best extimation
                               what have you

8   Classics skid
             on whetted lingo

                   an expensive spirit
                         is a shame to waste

            fog rolls up on
                  physical grammar

                         to shroud the imprint
                               of memory's trace

9   Abject realism
           titrates the intertext

               charmed specifics
                    of anarchic foam

          thus unmagicked
              by weight not volume

               the poem sinks
                    like a stone

10   Mons veneris
           vents its gist

               from amorous clamor
                    to scented sheen

          we who thirst for
              delight   not tedium

               swell with primate
                    dreams

11   Syntax maps
            the somatic splendor

                or heraldry of lickably
                    urbane parts

            she who signifies
                tribal displacement

                    outside language
                        it was raining

12   A nixed niche sequels
            a nominal shunt

                at vespers with dibs
                    on sufferance

            twice-tweaked angels
                writhe and tithe

                    to a gizmo's
                        sermonific sass

13   Labor parses
            pain and gain

                another day older
                    and deeper in debt

            pink slips blossom
                across the land

                when the bosses
                    pop a sweat

14   Spectral analysis
            vacates meaning

                famine relief goes
                    door to door

            in a gnostic scam
                a pseudomorph

                distributes arms
                    to the poor

15   The hellhound's warp
          belies its woof

               vocables strewn
                    in savvy riffs

         cadavers palaver
             while elites in heat

               clutch their info-
                    tainted glyphs

16   Gidget goes nova
          on the dyke matrix

               drawn to the tip
                    of a foreign tongue

         for which she yearns
             but was taught to spurn

               by decree
                    a biotic glitch

17   Mantic blueprints
            grid the analogy

                  glossed the undulant
                        pales in vitro

            a storied urge from
                  the post-Euclidian

                        ciphers the forecast
                              for the breeze

18   Quiddity jounced
            between shifts caps

                  the veridical I
                        and I in decision

            when the beer runs out
                  the plot thickens

                        like a full moon
                              over miasma

19   A logomancer
           spooked on spec

                 après a day's dose
                       dozes dazed

           who logicked else
                 his ache to thaw

                       by hand jive curbs
                             his household god

20   Death in mufti
           on a midnight creep

                 whistles up
                       a rented bride

           etudes bruit what
                 dull sense panders

                       ofay scrawls
                             Eurydicide

21   Wintering over in a wound
             that burgeons

                  the representative
                       skull at noon

            when the median strips
                 to whose delight

                       in your own words
                            name that tune

22   Condign data
             mined digs

                  the illiberal scruff
                       of private parts

            terminal rust
                 in a techno snit

                       tests its mettle
                            by fits and starts

23   Solid waste
              queries sundown

                 clouds clabbered
                        over auric stopes

              acquisitive glitz
                     at the chumporía

                     junk's bondage
                            a prophet's motif

24   Mélos says one thing
              follows another

                     juice and coffce
                            love in the house

              the sublime object
                     is nonreciprocal

                     therefore succor
                            the inflected indeed

25   Daily rushes
             the incommensurable

                    world writ small
                        at large

             shell mound with ash
                lit fastness

                    a prayer wheel
                        out-of-round

26   A rumorous breeze
             debrides the episteme

                    fluid dynamics of
                        the real as such

             the stain of love
                is upon the sheets

                    whipped lips delve
                        to divulge

27   Hep to the substrate
           dust appends

                celestial orders
                        beyond reproach

          whence ontology
              travels coach

                amidst a rout
                    and arousal

28   Birthed by edict
           errant Eros

              quivers a raffish
                  hatch of volts

          while simulacral
              lovers trill

              the chorus canticles
                  a peck

29   Ludic lust meets
                stray mandragora

                        break beats pump
                                their airborne knucks

                at the git-go Yo Po
                        jams with Macro

                                Fax in a ginkgo
                                        rap deluxe

30   A sober ghost
                is a dull fetish

                        a brutal beauty
                                spikes back

                twang and shimmy
                        tongue and groove

                                but it just don't
                                        work on you

31   Digitation
           stiffs the plural

                head tones margin
                    a capital crush

           points teased from
                the verb to deficit

                a firm rebuttal
                    in briefs

32   Chronic hunger
           networks dumpsters

                insolent echelons
                    mandate scraps

           lacking boots and
                their fabled straps

                tonight we dine
                    on pittance

33   Ego scriptor
           a signature destitution

           the habiliments
               of the page entire

      particle accelerants
           on opposite lock

            drive-by sonnets
                in scanthrax

34   Mind's largesse
           es muy tenebroso

           slippage ripples
              a neurobatic gliss

      estimados amigos
           intimates of what

            we were   traduced
               we were traduced

35   From hellish hutments
              pain's melisma

                   sings of slaughter
                           (light sweet crude)

         blooded quicks
              in a hard defile

                        collect their dead
                              with postage due

36   Gender mediates
              a weary continuum

                   who's who in situ
                        batched to sort

         by pulse and by proxy
              the dream that wakes

                        the caesura
                              madness bolsters

The Devil's Aria

And if occasionally a rhyme appeared
This was the illness but not the death.

— Laura (Riding) Jackson

1   Polis is spoils
         in mirrored shades

                 of works and days
                     an old refrain

             the sting of which
                 collective sweat

                     a cool breeze
                         don't explain

2   Bored by augury
         echoes of involute

                 yawps betoken
                     a mordant wit

             he whose last gaffe
                 gashed a vacuum

                     wherein the low ghost
                         glows 'not it'

3   Nature versus suture
          muchas gracias, amiga

               scars authenticate
                    a peccant skid

          the covenant bared
               to flesh such bones

                    whose rhythmic flexion
                         knowing tones

4   Blood work samples
          the lore of qualms

               tumescent dreams
                    of storied you

          excess graces
               sequent traces

                    plots a trocar
                         vents on cue

5   Art's high effort
        shadows small

           letters thick
               and thin impart

        lithic minions
           off the count

           obiter dictum –
               wrong from the start

6   A liminal logic
        from archon to agon

           mums the abuttal
               of kitsch and kin

        dressed to quell
           a phallus in furs

           un poco loco
               the diff avers

7   Anther and filament
                whet fate's warp

                        by virtue of grammar
                                a comely shill

                rich lips aptly
                        pursed in permeance

                                swell to horn
                                        or swill

8   Te Deum's tedium
                plus ça change

                        from audible squalor
                                to phatic scat

                if time is money
                        dead is broke

                                coinage to go
                                        at the idiomat

9 They want the story
    who want for song

      a lapse in praxis
        form portends

    from vocal folds
      to vibrant labes

       the thrum a tongue
        attuned attends

10 An Orphic doxy's
    post-hoc props

      at one with whom
       they cleave

    calamus astride
      the bitter acres

       contra naturam
        bound leaves

11   Wetware botches
            a batched sort

                or undead motley
                    in a burst cache

            reason in remission
                sweats the surfeit

                    scrolls a schizo-
                        mythic patch

12   Affinities fitted to
            blessed parentheses

                    once bespoke and
                        since been had

            you in translation
                by name encipher

                    restive revenants
                        on the pad

13   White noise cancels
        informed consent

               anxious flora
                    foliate the sticks

        cheap suits squeeze
           the public sphere

               extracting scratch
                    for a venal itch

14   Divas dive from
        the heights of fashion

               como se dice
                    to raise the dead

        while veteranos
           play the come

               the pavement plays
                    the spread

15   A sonic splice
        of doubtful provenance

        cold fusion
            chansons de gris

    in praise of rapture
        sound mind

        the sea within
            the sea

16   Bottle fatigue
        at Club Obsolescence

        blurs a rum wag's
            tale of flight

    lost in the language
        of all mute things

        Last Call conjures
            the dead of night

17   Oracles audit
              erotic auras

                     windblown errata
                         blot the moon

          a cognitive bypass
              downloads the lowdown

                     Big Stuff degausses
                         a caustic rune

18   The bottom line boogies
              to a dance of dearth

                     supply side out
                       a mouthpiece pleads

          from each according
              to his net worth

                     to each according
                         to his greed

19   The lens knows poses
                that animate the nation

                love for sale
                    in a one-way mirror

        harpies and loonies
            (a mistranslation)

                the future beckons
                    but not from here

20   Ambient sex seeks
            errant apogee

            a photogenic memory
                of lambent skin

        where tapers burn
            behind the eyes

                for love to light
                    a skull's chagrin

21 Who keeps the keys
           locks the locks

                    postmortem theory
                              dreams in braille

             façade by analogy
                        the numbskull factor

                         identity as index
                                   tooth and nail

22 Hair of the god
           between her teeth

                    la dama de noche
                              hits the stroll

             swing-shift bootay
                        elocutes thus

                         to anatomize
                                   goad and goal

23   A world of tricks
            no matter

                    where a book is
                            a taxable event

            virtual reality
                    includes us out

                        when the anomie within
                                is spent

24   Pointless to post
            enigmas to borders

                    bereft or belayed by
                            circumspection

            only heroes went twice
                    to the underworld

                        looking for love
                                or directions

Hard Science

You cannot solder an abyss with air

— Emily Dickinson

1   And so they came
            to the shining city

                    the burning city
                            the entropic city

            an arcanum devoted
                    to punishing choices

                            as ingress of fact
                                    as desolation

2   Steal away
            or start steppin'

                    magnetic North
                            perchance to dream

            a social fabric
                    of many colors

                            cut and stitched
                                    on the bias

3   Gilded phalloi
        in a rare heroic

            greet the dawn
                at river's edge

       where civic virtue
           at a deep discount

             lights these straits
                and narrows

4   If how things work
        is what things are

            demolition is progress
              watch our dust

    while elders raise
        their hands to praise

            a landmark writ
              in rubble

5 The verb seeking
    to be was

      to animate not
        to annihilate

   in those days
     they had eyes

      for visions – keep
        the peace, Bozo

6 A Pyrrhic hard-on
    tops the charts

     low-rent booty
       in high erotic guise

   such is the curator
    of scar's surmise

      coming home from
       a psychometric binge

7   East of the sun
          the utopic choir

                    musicates to the tears
                         of things

               thus *if you break it*
                    you buy it sings

                         the eponymous widget
                              in falsetto

8   The climate they fled
          was never the weather

                    but the very streets
                         they walked on

               who cut their losses
                    burned their crosses

                         and beat their boards
                              into time-shares

9   Unspeakably modern
        by choice or chance

          how a city dies
            when you leave it

      while raggedy revenants
        sweep the streets

           for the inclement angel
             of the supplement

10   A dope climate
       summer and a spoon

         easy livin' from
           pipe to mouth

      where the fish are high
        and the cotton's jumpin'

          and it's sleepy time
           up South

11   Designer shackles
            ready to wear

                cerements sewn
                    from bloody rags

        a Glock's spiel
            requiescat tolls

                for a populace
                    bagged and tagged

12   History's fables
            will not suffice

                to rcvive these products
                    of chaos and ice

        as if anything native
            to this place

                could grow here –
                    spin that, Doctor

13   Justice gropes
            a hung jury

                    the fixed idea dozes
                            the defense rests

            incremental ironies
                    glaze the galleries

                            a gag rule chomps
                                    at the bit

14   Bread and slaughter
            a plenary indulgence

                    from venture capital
                            to virtual cash

            snake eyes herald
                    a new regime

                            of passwords
                                    and panache

15   The city tires
                of the poet

                        his idylls of love
                                and death

                the bare limbs of
                        trees in winter

                        the young
                                in early spring

16   Erect racemes
                grainy flow of lichen

                        ranunculus set
                                in Perpetua

                the melody mimics
                        the order of bloom

                                whose quitclaim
                                        frees das Ding

17   Tangible assets
               wow and flutter

                   legs for days
                         and endless nights

          a karmic sutra
               in erotic sexameter

                   or hardcore dithyramb
                     early to rise

18   The mirror decodes
               a mated pair

                   autonomy hums
                         in the tain

          a toccata for tongue
               in a red sector

                   my one vice
                     my other

19   The page demanded
        a topology of drift

            morphs in section
                fleeced verbatim

        for a few gross
            of broken lines

            or a full-blown
                recantation

20   Stones in my passway
        the prosody of place

            refractive in season
                to make this plaint

        and raise a mojo
            hand to paint

            a griot's grigri
                in grisaille

21   Memory racks
             the geosyllabary

                   limbs inscribed on
                          catastrophic stone

             impaired faculties
                   gloss the ejecta

                          Vesuvial sunrise
                                archival ash

22   Urban renewal
             'buked and scorned

                   the eminent domain
                          of ghosts

             whose music echoes
                   coast to coast

                          from the shadows of
                                the alleys of   Paradise

23   A vacant lot
            a piece of string

                  memento mori
                        these foolish things

            a tree where late
                  the Yardbird sings

                        in the aureate
                              aura of orature

24   The tree falls
            or it doesn't

                  you hear it
                        or you don't

            contingency plans
                  a party or a wake

                        either way
                              it's dead

Parker's Mood

a tune is a kind of tautology

— Ludwig Wittgenstein

1   Daily the departed
        get closer

               not to be dismissed
                      by tough luck

          against all deliberate
               refinement of thought

                    change the record
                        drive the car

2   Rebop drops
        a stitch in time

               a fraught frequency's
                    panned gloss

          the maestro demands
               his pound of flesh

                  and a garland of
                    sheer obliquity

3   April in Paris
            a season in hell

                    some such gamut
                        of teenage bunk

            under the lash
                of a votive tongue

                        whose veriest form
                            follows funk

4   Moonlight waxes
            spring's vacuity

                    gleams and wanes
                        like eyeball sex

            devolves from clouds
                and rain to sweat

                        extracting heat
                            from the tumidity

5   Memory displaces
          more than it admits

                    mythemes bind
                         what they ensnare

               dead letters bask
                    in rhetorical weather

                         torch songs light
                              the eidetic air

6   Midnight special
          amber waves

                    triple filtered and
                         stored in staves

               the vox pop shops
                    for boss tops

                         but the prize is
                              on the bottom

7   Camp census
            the flambeau division

                    epic preachments
                            in festive drag

            reprise da capo
                    the zero-sum blues

                    then dance
                            the millennial rag

8   At night with all
            its hinges hung

                    the Pleiades geeze
                            before their set

            while backroom boys
                    order take-outs

                    to hegemonize
                            their bets

9   Rolling thunder
        posts no bills

           from terra infirma
              to the killing floor

      hamlet pacified
        by lone ranger

           whose muzzle flash
              lights the score

10   Ballistic waves
        elude the censorium

           hardly no wobble
              in online sex

      an imprecation
        cigarro con huevos

           bodes instanter
              a counter hex

11   Gradus ad veneris
               the slippery slope

                   from marble to marvel
                        a Galatean tease

             whose form informs
                 what dreams made flesh

                   drifts and burns
                       on semic seas

12   Skank in excelsis
               jukes the quad

                   the amative absolute
                       parsed in gloom

             a demotic embouchure's
                 gross récit

                   leaks in synopsis
                       from tome to tomb

13   Star thistle blooms
               under razor wire

                    free-range topoi
                              built to suit

               first the delay
                    then the alarm

                         and then the dance
                              of the postulants

14   Spare the rod
               greet the lightning

                    out of nowhere
                         la musique savante

               a rare monster
                    stalks the toy box

                         conjured there
                              by the onliest monk

15   Message deleted
        by natural selection

            whose rhetoric retails
                wholesale slaughter

      if less is more
        one is many

            pressed flowers
                in leaves of grass

16   Measured grief
        whose accents image

            staged convictions
                staggers home

      classic veins
        in eternity ornament

            the burnout
                or scratch of ages

17   A willful child
           in a woeful world

              goes to school
                 on Bird and Diz

         then dreams beneath
            that scofflaw tree

                 whose first fruit
                    knowledge is

18   Want for want
           whose needs bleed proof

              bad love's litmus
                 black and blue

         raw flesh is better than
            none sing the angels

                 what was it like
                    for you

19   Desire exacts
              a hard-won truce

                    from the fictive fervor
                        of a fabled beauty

          whose lust inscribes
              the laureate of lack

                    within her radius
                        or radiance

20   Carrier waves
              in holophrase

                    redact the hymnal
                        from its hymns

          a wanton por nada
              ebbs and flows

                    in a tango of
                        phantom limbs

21 Acceptable losses
          actuarial bliss

                Myrmidons sprung from
                      blood on demand

          half-mad have-nots
                half in love with

                      the whips and chains
                            of command

22 Fleshly tremors
          vex the periphery

                lexemes augur
                      form's decor

          to tongue the anomaly
                lip the bridge

                      a gold tooth pleads
                            a riddled core

23   The head of state
           a cerebral insult

                 anabatic evil
                      synaptic blight

           quando il pesce puzza
                 puzza della testa

                 unlimited drift
                      to the Right

24   Madness insists
           on its definitions

                 anaesthetic distance
                      out-of-body pain

           the ghosts are hungry
                 and we're lunch

                 hand me down
                      my walkin' cane

25   Strode modes
        phase the egress

           poste restante
              the sea's swell

      a bard's code keyed
         to pricked ears

            an allegory's prompt
               allegro

26   Breached sectors
        gorged on dyads

          hot blood buffers
            an evident itch

      soup in extremis
        narrates the ghost

           and then went down
             with the ship

27   Waveforms mark
            conceptual wakes

                  raw decibels
                        flog the street

            to paint by numbers
                  past their prime

                        melody's assassin
                              in profile

28   A temblor's tutorial
            chthonic phonics

                  phallic milk
                        in a matrix of surds

            coaxing scratch
                  from the jinxomatic

                        to put some English
                              on it

29   Thighs' down glistens
              in a photon stream

                      stepping down from
                             a dream machine

              technology transfers
                     the Bernoulli effect

                            into classic skirts
                                   that cling

30   Indentured reams
              semantify the schema

                      who bring the noise
                             the stays noise

              ramped to deflect
                     the cryptoplex

                            from beauty
                                   to exempla

31   A squall of demons
            vectored plumb

                    summons shades
                            from true North

            signal fires
                    abet depiction

                    at the fierce funnel
                            of the referent

32   From bedrock straight
            to venereal soil

                    the tune's image
                            beginning to end

            behind closed doors
                    in a club at dawn

                    Pan sops gin while
                            the band plays on

33   Body heat tempers
            a mental chill

                    dolce far niente
                            up in smoke

            not for nothing
                    we could live with that

                        but for that
                            we are bespoke

34   Though few or none
            attend these songs

                    for what they are
                            or come to be

            some may discern
                    among pebbles

                        polished work
                            of the sea

35   To write a republic
        from landfall to landfill

            immigrant dreams
                in motley array

        where storefront faith
            in name-brand gods

            bespeaks a history
                of decay

36   Atrocities blossom
        in the garden of immunity

            mass graves open
                above the fold

        while tyrants tally
            bones in situ

            and turn the dead
                to gold

Phase Rule

we are suspended in language

— Niels Bohr

1   Day breaks on the last man standing

memory factors blood from a stone
oblique benisons   a topology of mourning

when the sun rises   it comes up red

2   From chemical bond to chimerical weave

the fatality of a distance that closes
and comes at last to what was first

bred out and then bled out

3   Portions of this childhood were prerecorded

in the far-flung nursery of stars
a warp in space-time shrouds the infinitive

to see that my grave is kept clean

4   The bent day sings its declination

if you lived here you'd be dead by now
lost in the penitential logic of ruins

where the chill is father to the flame

5   Reason's regent retrofits the dreamscape

     angelic accents explicate the lack
     ghosted notes requite their begetting

     the masque is a series of masks

6   Dead leaves drift on parochial breezes

     local tongues tell the local time
     destiny's dispatch duly inscribed

     in the annals of a blue-sky scam

7   Silence shapes a mordant remix

     phantom entries   throated gaps
     in time each name discerns its root

     in the death of the thing it names

8   Impossible music   visible scars

     in sintered chords from beaten brass
     the anarchy of production masks

     an infinitely small vocabulary

9   Last words pass from hand to mouth

     the mechanics of emphasis   blanc de blancs
     clear eyes hear what's read by ear

     as toxic zeroes in solution

10   Bel canto nullities hedged on account

     their indentured outcome to encrypt
     one-time ciphers from the axis of digression

     to the axis of perturbation

11   Chaos delights in dreams of order

     quondam et futurus   on Lethe's shore
     while structural theorems are sent in lieu

     of girders to rut with giants

12   The order of battle (in nomine patris)

     parses (et filii) the human remains
     displaced personae of poetic extraction

     but only the ghost is holy

13   Chronic oblations repo the repros

          from restricted access to mystical conceit
          an explanatory fiction   elective trauma

          or commotion resurrected in futility

14   Eros absconditus   extant glyphs

          in the absence of visible means
          an indexical scherzo cribs the manifest

          content of his emprise

15   Agency disperses in real time

          tools that are no good require more skill
          the product of these uncertainties

          is the constant of our faith

16   A cupped harp conjures two trains running

          flat to the correlate   nowhere fast
          the edict says what the exile knows

          the point of departure is to leave

17   Vultures circle a corporate campus

      deer trails eulogize terraced hills
      beneath the gaze of an orphaned libido

      aloft in a corner office

18   With patient syllables Our Lady of Sorrows

      dispels the falsities of each next dawn
      not least the happy measure of our days

      as facts in the fictions we have lived

19   This week's novices weed the residuals

      culled from the shadows of their doubt
      a constant curriculum of Sturm und Drang

      to turn this mother out

20   Penile dementia   tricked-out riffs

      a botched apex in the cryptic sublime
      under the sign of a genital economy

      whose heat is adjunct to its light

21   The gray scale weighs a season's affect

      on condition of anonymity
      advanced decomposition (une pratique sauvage)

      remember to breathe when you dream

22   Majuscules pledge their antic allegiance

      to a bitmap of Trajan's Column
      while cut stone crumbles to pixel dust

      the code sleeps in the sun

23   Virtual warfare   opposable thumbs

      the necropolis or empire in repose
      whose acolytes orbit an urban agora

      in lockstep to limn their theodicy

24   Flat-earth follies in the moral menagerie

      face time chronicles a horse's ass
      rot's mute racket   the anti-lyric

      the horizon placed in evidence

25   New years gone into old habits

     singular enough for piecework
     heir to a tombstone disposition

     born of a graveyard mind

26   Attitude adjustment   a three-second burn

     on the stump between ways and means
     what one word won't where any will do

     correct me if I'm not wrong

27   Shadows bruise a virgin palette

     two tears set the margins of this grief
     the subject stalked by a predicate felon

     to the ragged edge of the page

28   Prosthetic prosody   anaerobic angst

     descants the romance of the road
     a deceptive cadence in digital delay

     cloud   chamber   music

29   Gender adorns a red dilemma

       in the polynomial perverse
       from stepwise melody to cemetery plot

       recumbent roses   rampant thorns

30   A rogue wave mounts a demiquaver

       for a money shot by proxy
       while anachronous others chart the depths

       of ancestral ruts to drown in

31   Eyes surmise what's bared in the scan

       paratactic rebates   pyrotechnic hooks
       mind-forged manacles of simulacra

       to gird the republic of the dead

32   Hell is for seekers the haven sought

       by the fires of the city of the poem called thought
       gleaned in the glow of game scintilla

       gone to glad extinction

33   The world as will   a double negative

bares its device in the court of miracles
this is the interval where nothing precedes

the nothing that surely follows

Dark Matter

less language than music,
less syntax than songs of words

— Hélène Cixous

1   By stealth and by starlight
          to traverse these confines
               withal their harmonies
                    may be infinite   as desire is
                         and is not   disaster   as
              the subject is   a void
   of dispersion   without
          portfolio   forever
             mapping the distances
                these confines are
                    and decline to admit

2   Fractals on the B side
          of the geologic record
             convene to illumine
                an astigmatic score
                    leading the conductor
             to vacate the podium
  and approach
        a window or abyss
            of importunity
              through or to which
                 lightning bolts

3   The low ghost posits
            a fire in the hole
                    whence to extract
                            the prima materia
                                    that is the currency
                of fools   this
    or so we imagine
            is a reckoning   as if
                    there were anything
                            beyond consumption
                                    after the fire is gone

4   The mortal remains
            of our due diligence
                    impel us to canvass
                          this ruined landscape
                                to compose these
                  gathering clouds   beneath
    whose aegis DJ Phat Wha
        clogs the bloggeries
                  with utter prepostrophes
                        and a self-serve soupçon
                            of hypoplastic jive

5   A calculus raised on
            paradox displays of all
                that is the minim
                      of all that is and isn't
                              perceptible from here –
                for all we know
     it might be paradise
            whose fictive brilliance
               fails to pierce
                    the maximal dark
                      of our days

6   Huddled for warmth
            against the insurgent
                ghost wind with
                    its patriarchal chill
                          nerve ends burn
              at each next strophe's
   cut and course from
           borrowed longings
             to the proximate verge
                of a fatal technê
                    that signals their demise

7   Viva la muerte
          though none the wiser
               Morpheus morphs
                    the available stock
                        of all too human bits
            thus to extend
   or limn a genealogy
         from party favors
            to party discipline
               who's your daddy?
                   what's your line?

8   Invention falters in a glut
         of dittos   gravity gathers
            extruded days
               and the implicate order
                  of prevailing winds
            determines the praxis
   of hand and eye
         there to display and
            sum our misprisions
               for which no assembly
                  is required

9   Sifting the middens
                by epochal inches
                      for the prodigal spirit
                              of sublimity –
                                      to every demand
                    its hecatomb   to every lack
its desire – where the least
              we can do
                    or sacrifice to
                          is too much
                                and never enough

10   Labor labors to escape
              its end and means to
                    annotate every star
                        that underwrites its fate –
                            it is at best a wintry mix
                  of chores and chattel
whose bitter repertoire
              spurs the warlords
                  to table futurity
                    while the crocus
                        publishes its dissent

11   Of the world
        and its double
            kaput in situ
                iterable elements tally
                    the years now lost
           to the memory
    of moments –
        as if all that remained
            of the will to change
                is a codicil that says
                    we are dead

12   The elders recall
        the historical subject
            stuck in traffic
                on the Via Negativa
                    a patrimony lost
           to a discourse of rights
    that can only
        serve to defer
            the arrival of
                hope and the trope
                    that it rode in on

13 From bread and water
        to body and blood
                (a metabolic gloss
                        on a transubstantial
                                endgame)
                prayerful regimes
    of variform ilk
        claim each malediction
                as the registered trademark
                        of a value-added scourge
                                in simulcast

14 Refractive to
        the diurnal blight
            their daily walk inscribes
                    vertiginous shimmers of
                            shot gray silk drape
                modernism's skin of glass –
    where from his aerie
        the local boss-clone
                posts an agenda in
                    a pixelated bottle on
                            a bootleg plasma screen

15 A strange hysteresis
    exists in the transport
      of language by language
        to language –
          where squalor breeds
      necrotic stank
   distilled from common
    if unheroic stains
      and slyly rebranded
        for a tourist economy
          as the latest eau de ville

16 Unable to combat
    the inertia of language
      anxious biophobes
        search for signs
          of life amidst
     the life of signs – e.g.
   ribbons of exurban asphalt
    that link faux châteaux
      and designer trees
        to define the ambit
          of a cul-de-sac

17   Homo economicus
             trades on denizens
                  increasingly inured
                         to the cost of living
                                in rank immiseration –
             which they tithe
      to the gods of chance
             they imagine favor
                the sacral smoke
                    that rises from
                        their hovels

18   A caress brought forward
             from childhood's ledger
                  soothes raw flesh and
                      buffs what's left
                         of sacrificial stone
                there to indite
      in the brutal light
             of consensual amnesia
                what little remains
                    to show or tell what
                        make-believe believes

19   If cessation of desire
                is the end of suffering
                        it is to that end
                                we suffer   and yet
                                        we can find no
                        forwarding address
        for those who exist
                on the margins
                        of a State that
                                extols each death
                                        for cause

20   Funereal rites redress
                no wrong   though we find
                        ourselves in a different
                                century in a different part
                                        of the object world
                        where even the terrible
        war is different
                and nothing we suffer
                        the loss of is lost
                                until it is lost
                                        to memory

21 The lethal seed
in the mise-en-scène
encrypts the grammar
of a green profusion
(why? because it can
because it cannot
help itself) while here
in a grove of selfsame
difference icons of
renewal faintly flicker
flare and fade away

22 As bodies at work
on bodies of work
we are heirs to the empire
of the alphabet
we were born to
and which escorts us
to the archive of bones
unable to name there
what we have become
or to praise the silence
that surrounds us

Null Set

The book is often described as a tomb

— Jacques Derrida

I   In the cloistered light

of a winter sun
the elements speak

of things undone

while a singularity
or ill-starred die

is cast in futurity

elsewhere than art
unable to recall

the other it is

and cannot know
itself to be   thus

that forgetfulness

that is the human
that defines itself

in extremity

2   Tired of appearance

and disappearance
the caesura marks

what might be

otherwise   estranging
and estranged

between tropes

whose mitered
edges mock

the Pyrrhic

muthos of presence
that was lost

from the start

and played no part
in whatever art

might claim it

3   Beyond knowledge

and the reach of eyes
the horizon retreats

to untold revels

while an aging exile
empties his pockets

before the walls

of the visible city
where a bevy

of mathemes

attendant shades
and a corpus

of glacial

derivatives confirm
his departure

is his bequest

4   Unlikely

      as it seems the years
      carry over

      to burden

      the topos that
      we call home

      to which we address

      these psalms
      of negation

      in which we encrypt

      as remnants
      and revenants

      all that remains

      of our mother
      tongue   at home

      in no man's land

5   Not the embrace

     but the encounter
     is decisive

     where the word

     and the wordless
     arise as from death

     and meet to invoke

     a topology of being
     whose form

     is a form

     of love made plain
     by what spirits are

     or say they are

     when hauntology
     interpellates

     phonology

6   Difficult as ever

    to speak of paradise
    or the errant angel

    of the supplement

    that curve of breast
    those canted hips

    whose contours

    in their stark relief
    delineate our days

    such are the signs

    of a dispossession
    we endure

    as in an anguish

    of mortality and take
    as emblems

    to our wounds

7 The narrative founders

  on mythic scarps
  Outis the cognomen

  of an ontic rift

  where uncanny blossoms
  run a gauntlet of air

  and open the living

  past to risk
  not least the risk

  of that disaster

  wherein the memory
  of what

  will have been

  proscribes any present
  occurrence

  to memory

8   As above   so below

even in hell
the dead keep busy

given that thought

is no longer thought
of death nor death

the death of thought

and we who traffic
with the dead

breathe their words

as if our own
and lend to them

a living tongue

to tell and to remind
ourselves of what

we've left undone

9   A little madness

goes a long way
though every step

be a further step

into madness –
and to know this

whatever it is to know

is to know this
in advance –

in light of which

we find what is
(as it is) impedes

what might be

otherwise   unless
we retreat

from madness

10   Breath equivocates

      where once it praised
      a tradition that lives

      on borrowed time

      the figure at issue
      in the nexus of art

      is the continuity

      of song made strange
      which is

      not nothing

      but for that nothing
      it would fill

      in making

      whatever remains
      to be made there

      in its name

II   The wind in the wires

is also song
of which no words

survive

as what was written
must now be

written

over (and over)
in the archive

of an image

that is not a song
but a cipher

addressed

to the many
we are

that more shall be

About the Author

TED PEARSON (1948) was born and raised in Palo Alto, California. Early studies in liturgical music, modernism, and jazz led him to poetry in the mid 1960s. He attended Vandercook College of Music, Foothill College, and San Francisco State University. His many books of poetry include *Extant Glyphs: 1964-1980* (Singing Horse, 2014), *An Intermittent Music: 1975-2010* (Chax, 2016), and *The Coffin Nail Blues* (Atelos, 2016). A new volume, *After Hours*, is forthcoming from Singing Horse. He co-edited *Bobweaving Detroit: The Selected Poems of Murray Jackson* (Wayne State UP, 2004). He co-authored *The Grand Piano: An Experiment in Collective Autobiography* (This / Mode A, 2006-2010) in ten volumes. And his essays have been widely published, notably in *Poetics Journal*. A two-part conversation with Luke Harley appears in *Jacket2*. It focuses on the evolution of *An Intermittent Music*. After leaving the Bay Area in 1988, Pearson lived in Ithaca, Buffalo, and Detroit. He now lives in southern California, where he is adjunct faculty at the University of Redlands.

About CHAX

Founded in 1984 in Tucson, Arizona, Chax has published nearly 200 books in a variety of formats, including hand printed letterpress books and chapbooks, hybrid chapbooks, book arts editions, and trade paperback editions such as the book you are holding. In August 2014 Chax moved to Victoria,Texas, and is presently located in the University of Houston-Victoria Center for the Arts, which has generously supported the publication of *An Intermittent Music*, which has also received support from many friends of the press. Chax is an independent 501(c)(3) organization which depends on support from various government and private funders, and, primarily, from individual donors and readers.

Recent and current books-in-progress include T*he Complete Light Poems*, by Jackson Mac Low, *Life–list*, by Jessica Smith, *Andalusia*, by Susan Thackrey, *Diesel Hand*, by Nico Vassilakis, *Dark Ladies*, by Steve McCaffery, *What We Do: Essays for Poets*, by Michael Gottlieb, *Limerence & Lux*, by Saba Razvi, *Entangled Bank*, by James Sherry, *Arrive on Wave: Collected Poems*, by Gil Ott, and more books to come.

You may find *chax* online at http://chax.org/